MW01078617

ISBN-13: **978-1979069625**

ISBN-10: **197906962X**

Amy Roberts

Email: amy@raisingarrows.net

Facebook: http://www.facebook.com/RaisingArrows

Twitter: @raising_arrows

Google+: https://plus.google.com/u/0/+AmyRoberts/posts

Pinterest: http://www.pinterest.com/amyraisingarrows/

YouTube: https://www.youtube.com/user/AmyRaisingArrows

Instagram: https://www.instagram.com/amyraisingarrows

TABLE OF CONTENTS

TABLE OF CONTENTS

BONUS CONTENT

INTRODUCTION

I have 10 children, 5 of whom are under the age of 8. Some days I wake up and the next thing I know, it's bedtime! And some days bedtime seems light-years away. *(can I get an amen?!)*

But one thing remains constant - someone always needs me.

When you have a lot of little ones, it can feel like there isn't enough of you to go around. You meet yourself coming and going most days. Often you wish you simply had more hours in the day...or a maid...or both.

This book is your guide to sanity. It won't magically give you more hours...or a maid...but it will give you practical ideas to find more time. Time to guide, discipline, love and enjoy your little ones!

CHAPTER 1

Setting Yourself up for Success

CHAPTER 1

I have one word for you -

EXPECTATIONS.

That one word can make or break you as a mother. Your expectations can be reasonable or irrational. They can be based on Biblical truth or other people's opinions. They can be unique to your family or built on comparisons and guilt.

Your expectations must line up with what the Lord has planned for YOUR family, YOUR children, YOUR life in order for you to truly be successful as a mother.

We all know it isn't wise to compare ourselves with others (2 Corinthians 10:12). We all know how dangerous it is to have unrealistic expectations and/or take advice from people not walking the same road we are. We all know we must stay focused on Christ and not veer to the right or to the left as we look to see what others are doing. Yet, time and again, we fall into the trap of thinking we are failing and looking to a method to save us.

Perhaps that is why you bought this book.

You were hoping it would solve all of your problems and make you a joyful mommy full of energy, sunshine, and tea parties. But, that's not what you will find here.

First of all, let me point you to Christ. HE is perfect. I am not. I need a Savior - mostly to save me from myself. I am THE

3

Setting Yourself up for Success

WORST at wanting methods to fix me. I am THE WORST at hoping a book will fix all my problems once and for all. But the truth is that mankind is woefully broken, and apart from Christ I am nothing.

What you WILL find in this book are ideas, hope, and REASON-ABLE expectations and admonitions. I won't try to convince you I have it all together and that if you implement everything I say, you will have the perfect life because that would be a big, fat lie.

What I will give you is a Titus 2 perspective as a mom who has been there - for nearly 20 years. I was encouraged, guided, and challenged by older women along my journey. They weren't trying to make me more like them, but rather more like Christ. That is what I want for you - focus in the right place, expectations that line up with the Bible, and practical tools to help you be the family God made you to be!

So, set yourself up for success by letting go of other people's expectations for your family - perceived or real. Whether it be your mom, your mother-in-law, the lady down the street, or the blogger on the internet - none of them are living YOUR life. You do not answer to them. You answer to Christ. And when it is all said and done, the only expectation you should have is to hear, "Well done."

CHAPTER 2

Systems for the Stressors

Systems for the Stressors

Take a moment to think over your typical morning. What things stick out in your mind as the worst part of your morning or the things that never seem to get done that really NEED to get done?

Those things need systems.

For instance, is laundry all over the bedroom, all over the bath-room, all over the house? Put a laundry basket in the hallway and that becomes your holding place for dirty laundry. Then, come up with a system for actually getting the laundry washed, dried and put away. Our current system (because no system works forever) is as follows:

16 year old daughter washes 2 loads each on Monday and Wednesday. 13 year old daughter washes 2 loads each on Tuesday and Thursday. My 19 year old son washes 2 loads on Friday, and I wash as much as possible over the weekend. The clothes are folded to individual tubs. We call each child to put away his or her tub - usually during Tidy Time around 4pm.

It's a system, and currently, it works! It lessens the stress of laundry because it is a no-brainer. Is it Monday? Then, laun-dry is Megan's responsibility. Wash 2 loads, dry 2 loads, sort 2 loads into tubs, call the kids, they put them away and return the tubs, and we are DONE!

Now, I realize I have older kids to pitch in, but that doesn't mean you can't find a system that works for you with only littles.

CHAPTER 2

When I only had littles, I didn't need to wash every day. In fact, for a time, I could get by with only washing once a week - on Monday. I would wash all the loads, dry them, put them away, and sit back and ignore the laundry for the rest of the week!

So, here's the key takeaway from this conversation - think through your entire day and consider what parts and pieces of your day are stressors and could benefit from a system.

Here are a few ideas:

- a morning system to combat the first-thing-in-the-morning craziness
- a bath system
- a table chore system
- regular tidy up times
- laundry systems
- meal time systems
- shopping systems
- and the list goes on!

If it is stressing you out, give it a system!

And yes, for a few years here, you are the main one making the system run. Eventually, you will have some kiddos to train. And one day, I promise, you will have big kids to implement your systems!

You will find much of this book is built around the notion of systems and what you can do to simplify the big things, so you have more time with the little ones in your life. The more you can put on autopilot, the less stressed out you will be!

CHAPTER 3

Good Mornings

Good Mornings

The phrase "woke up on the wrong side of the bed" takes on a whole new meaning when you have little ones. Your morning either starts out stellar or starts out stinky. There is no in between.

You won't always get stellar mornings, but I can offer you some useful tools and tips for having less stinky mornings. Consider where you are in your motherhood journey, and implement the following suggestions accordingly...

Scenario 1
Your youngest is an infant

A new baby in the house always requires adjustment, and some babies require more than others. Baby #6 didn't require nearly the adjustment Baby #7 did for me. Baby #7 was colicky. I wasn't able to go back to homeschooling and home cooking as soon as I had with most of the others. I had to focus much of my energy on him for the better part of 4 months. It was tough, and I was tired.

Mornings were for sleeping as long as I could, and then nursing as long as he needed. Truth be told, this is how my mornings go with most of my infants. In order to make the house run as smoothly as possible while I care for the newest baby, I put these tools and systems in place...

1. Easy breakfast
This is the season of cereal, protein shakes, and bars. It's toast

and fruit. It's milk in smaller containers and juice in single serv-
ings. It's anything the older children can get by themselves or
help each other get. It's easy, easy, easy - no mom involvement,
except for the occasional instruction given from a comfortable
chair nearby. And when someone from church or your play-
group says, "What can I bring you for a meal after baby comes?"
say BREAKFAST! (Why does no one bring breakfast?!)

2. Morning Chores
Having a set of morning chores will make your mornings MUCH
smoother. Yes, you will need to remind your children about
morning chores for oh, the next 18 years or so, but once your
children know what is expected of them when you say, "Do your
morning chores," it will send them into automatic mode. However, DO NOT make morning chores a huge list of to-do's. Keep it
super simple. You could even make a chart with pictures to tell
them exactly what they need to do.

maybe 3

Here's an example of our Morning Chore List:
*   Get dressed
*   Brush teeth
*   Make bed
*   Tidy room
*   Put laundry in hallway

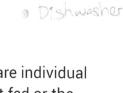

Three
BCD
Beds
Clothes
Dishwasher

I don't have any chores on our morning list that are individual
chores, but if you need something done like a cat fed or the
dishwasher unloaded or a bathroom wiped down, simply assign
it to a capable child (even if they are only capable of doing a

semi-good job) and make sure they know it is part of their morning chores.

3. A Mom Basket
For nearly all of my babies, I have had something that could be called a Mom Basket. It has evolved over the years, but it has always served the same purpose - to make Mom's life easier during the infant days.

When I had my second child, it was the bottom drawer in her dresser. I would sit in a comfy chair in her bedroom to nurse her, and my little son would sit at my feet and rifle through that drawer full of toys and books just for him. Later, it would become a literal basket - shallow and rectangular - full of diapers, wipes, pen and paper, tissues, toddler books, a few toys, and my water bottle.

It was the place for everything I might need while confined to the chair feeding baby. It was a centralized location for Mom's Stuff. To make your own Mom Basket, pick a good location, choose things that are regularly needed by you and the children, and find a way to store them.

4. No early morning plans
No early morning appointments. No early morning playdates. No early morning lessons, grocery shopping expeditions, or meetings.
Late morning? Sure. Early morning - don't even go there.

CHAPTER 3

When you have a new baby, mornings are a grab bag of crazy. You have no idea what your night before will be like, so avoid a whole heap of stress by staying home.

Scenario 2
You are pregnant

(See Scenario 1)

Scenario 3
Mostly toddlers and preschoolers

A house full of toddlers and preschoolers is sort of like running a zoo. They need to be fed, and they need to have boundaries. Here are a few ideas to give them both:

1. Breakfast and Bible
Serve up a simple breakfast and a healthy dose of Scripture. Get a good Story Bible or read from your own Bible. Little hands and mouths are busy, and getting the Word of God in them (and you!) first thing is a great way to start off your day! Don't try to read too much at a time or you may begin to lose them. The key is to keep it steady and consistent.

2. Morning Chores
Remember to create those morning chores! (see Scenario 1)

Scenario 4
A few bigs, a few littles

Good Mornings

As you move from only littles into the land of big kids, you will slowly feel your load lighten. You aren't the only playmate, the only entertainment, the only helper. Now is the time to seize the day!

1. Assign buddies
My older girls take turns caring for the toddler in the morning. This includes changing her diaper, getting her dressed, and getting her something to eat for breakfast. My middle son helps his younger brothers put away their laundry. We try to instill in our children an understanding that we should help those who need us, and at home, those in need are those younger than ourselves.

2. Morning Chores
Are you noticing a pattern? (see Scenario 1)

3. Do some Prep Work for the day
When you have some bigs who can help out in the mornings, it gives you time to prep your day for success. Read in your Bible, make lists for the day, make phone calls or answer emails, pay bills. Remember to set a limit on how much time you are spending online (or avoid it altogether!), so you don't end up frittering your entire morning away because you "accidentally" ended up on Facebook!

Hopefully, you have found some ideas to get your morning started off right! I also highly recommend you create some traditions around your morning time. For me, that means a cup of coffee with almond milk creamer, my Bible, and our current read-aloud. If I get nothing else done in the morning, at least I've had my coffee and my Jesus.

CHAPTER 4

Good Nights

CHAPTER 4

It might seem a bit illogical to jump from morning to night in one chapter, but let's face it, that's often what my day feels like - I wake up, I go to bed - rinse and repeat. And more often than not, my "good morning" depends on my "good night." So, there... makes perfect sense!

I have to admit getting kids to bed has been a struggle for me since about baby number 6. When the kids were all little, I just threw them all in bed at the same time. When I started having bigs and littles, bedtime got complicated. The 10 year old did not want to go to bed at the same time as the 3 year old, and the 7 year old was convinced she could stay up as long as the 10 year old. It's easy to find yourself in nighttime negotiations, but try to avoid that mess because you won't win and they will "get to" stay up later "arguing" their point. It's time for mom to show a little tough love.

First of all, YOUR day needs an end. Just as a workday comes to an end, so must a mama day come to an end. The kitchen gets shut down, the lights get lowered, and tone of the home slows, and once the children are in bed and asleep, mom can take a deep day-ending breath - IF she has a plan in place.

If you do not put together an evening routine, your day will drag on well into the nighttime hours and beyond. As a mom of littles, you need all the energy you can spare, and that energy can often be found in a good night's sleep - even an interrupted night's sleep that begins at a decent time. So, how do you create a good night?

Good Nights

Start with a Bedtime Routine.

While a bedtime routine will not solve all your problems, it will make the evening predictable...and predictable is good. A good bedtime routine addresses as many of the "excuses" that cause kids to want to get out of bed, and it creates an atmosphere of "calm" that allows them to fall asleep more easily.
Here are the steps you can take to figure out your own Bedtime Routine:

1. Set a time for bed and work backward.
2. Remove as many distractions as you can.
3. Consider the trouble areas, and look for solutions.
4. Stay consistent, knowing this all takes time...lots of time.

Here is an example of a calming Bedtime Routine that has the goal of 8pm as bedtime:

7:15 pm - All electronic devices off (screens are a stimulant and can contribute to wakefulness)

7:30 pm - Diapers changed, pajamas on, and teeth brushed.

7:30 - 7:50 pm - Slow down time. (They can listen to audios, read, or play quietly. You could also put Family Worship Time in this slot.)

7:50 pm - Drinks and bathroom time. (small drink!)

CHAPTER 4

8:00 pm - Prayers and bed. (Make this time special if you can - sit in their room with them, give loves, tuck them in. If you are in a season when this isn't possible, do your best to make the act of putting them to bed a priority, no matter how brief it may be.)

Not every child gets the memo that Bedtime means SLEEP TIME, so if you have a wild child (like my current 4 year old), you may have to take some drastic measures. My drastic measures involve patrolling the hallway, shushing him to sleep, and some-times even sitting in his room to make sure he stays in bed. Someday he'll get the memo...I hope.

A Word on Sleep Training Babies

Some families are huge advocates for something called sleep training. It often involves allowing the child to cry until they go to sleep, often taking quite some time to get them to that place.

So, what is my take on sleep training?
I don't do it.

That is, I don't do it until my babies are older, and even then, I don't do it the way the "experts" tell you to do it.

I don't like the idea of trying to force an infant into a schedule. They find a natural rhythm and that rhythm typically includes a couple of middle-of-the-night feedings. If you are constantly bothered by their waking to eat, you will miss vital moments to cherish your little ones.

Good Nights

With one of my babies, I had a super comfy chair near where she slept and I would put on some soft music and sit in that chair and doze off while she nursed. Eventually, I would wake up and put her back in her crib, and head back to bed. I have very fond memories of listening to the music and my baby suckling in the stillness of the night hours.

But, there does come a time when I feel as if my babies need to start working toward longer stretches of sleep at night. Here are my personal guidelines for knowing if baby is ready for sleep training...

Is baby ready to sleep through the night? You have to make sure their tummies are full enough to make it through the night. You need to be able to differentiate between waking out of true hunger or waking out of habit.

Are there other factors? You have to make sure it isn't their diaper or the temperature of the room or Daddy snoring (yes, I'm serious!) that is waking them up at night. All these things can factor into their sleep/wake cycle at night.

Does baby have a way to self-soothe? Do they suck their thumb or take a pacifier? Do they have a lovey or a special blanket? Are they old enough to find a way to go back to sleep after waking up in the night? There isn't a "right age" for this, so use your discretion. For my children, this is rarely before 10 months of age, and my child with sensory issues didn't sleep through the night until she was 5!

CHAPTER 4

I also want to encourage you to really check your own bedtime attitude. I know when I am grumpy about how the children are sleeping (or not sleeping is more like it), I tend to be short-fused. I need to slow down and let the evening simmer and let my temper cool. One day I will be sorry I didn't relish and remember these days for what they are - just part of mothering.

CHAPTER 5

Afternoon Naps

CHAPTER 5

I recently spoke to a mom of several little ones who said, "I protect afternoon nap time with every ounce of my being." Afternoon naps can be a sanity saver for a tired mama, so guard them wisely!

Here are some ideas for creating a solid nap time routine:

Set a reasonable timeframe - Decide on the best time for naps based on the age of your child and when they start to get fussy in the afternoon. My two year old recently went from right-after-lunch naps to 2 o'clock naps. We made the transition when I realized she wasn't quite ready for a nap at 12:30pm, but was falling apart by 2:30pm.

Drown out noise - Use a fan, soothing music, or a noise machine.

Make nap time a consistent routine - You have a set time, in a set place, with a set order. It doesn't have to be elaborate, but a nice blanket and stuffed animal always helps. Beware of toys, however! Little ones are notorious for playing when they should be sleeping!

And if Mommy needs a nap, then by all means, take one! My personal caution is that you wait until they are asleep and then set a timer for yourself. I have also known mamas who locked themselves in the room with the nappers so that no one could sneak out, allowing her to sleep more peacefully.

What if my child no longer naps?

Afternoon Naps

The answer to this is simple - **Rest Time**. The rule is: You don't have to sleep, but you do have to REST. For our family, this means children who no longer nap go to their beds and lie down and read or play quietly with one toy. If I need the older ones to be separated from the younger ones, I will send them to other places in the house - behind chairs, on the couch, even in their closet with a comfy pillow and blanket!

Here are a few more ideas for creating a Rest Time Routine:

• Siesta - Directly after lunch and table chores, send the children to a quiet place for a break before starting up school again or heading out for afternoon expeditions.

• Room Time - This is a concept I learned from another mom of many. Teach your children to remain in their rooms for an allotted amount of time. This time can be maximized by putting together learning audios or requiring older children to read in their literature assignments.

• Mom Down Time - Use Rest Time to truly slow yourself down, mom! Don't try to do projects, or "maximize" your time by cramming a bunch of stuff into this time frame. You won't feel rested at all!

• Ambience and Atmosphere - Make Rest Time a special time with soft music, soft lighting, essential oil diffusers or candles. You can even take turns snuggling each of your little ones.

CHAPTER 6

Learning Time

CHAPTER 6

Every mom is a teacher, no matter how qualified (or unqualified) she feels. We naturally teach our children with the words we speak as we impart information to them about every day life. If you are a homeschool mom, you already plan to be intentional with your teaching, but even if you are not planning to home-school, you more than likely want to give your children a solid start to their academic career by teaching them things like their alphabet, numbers, colors, and more. But, how do you do this when you have a lot of littles?

I'm sure you probably have an ideal of what learning time *should* look like...

Let go of it.

That's right. Whatever you believe learning time should look like, it won't end up looking like that, and you will feel as if you failed, when really, you didn't.

When your children are small, learning time should be FUN! A stressed out mommy is NOT fun (just in case you were wonder-ing!). Sing the ABC's as you drive, count strawberries as you wash them, point out insects and plants, find simple projects to do, and HAVE FUN!

With that said, let me give you some guidance and ideas for integrating learning into your every day life with littles.

CHAPTER 6

Fill your home with educational play.
You don't need to spend a lot of money to have a home full of educational play! (Isn't that good news?!) You simply need to think outside the box. Children need open-ended playthings. They need a dress up box of REAL clothes, a bag of blocks, a few cheap dishes, enough stuffed animals to host a tea party, and TIME to play....plenty of time to play.

So many toys these days don't allow your child to be the author of the story. They tell your child what to think, they speak for your child, and they only have one or two functions rather than a treasure trove of endless ideas. Look for low-key toys - simple toys - even NON-toys (boxes, sticks and rocks, pots and pans).

Make books available to your little ones.
Designate a low shelf, a basket on the floor, a tote in their bedroom as a place for books they can access. Let them touch, taste, and "read" these books. Read to them from these books. Let them try to guess the ending. And when you have read it 400 times, let them finish the sentences. Buy your own library or go to your local library and start filling their little heads with words!

Have special "school" activities.
Most toddlers and preschoolers I know all want to "do school." Put together easy busy bags, toddler boxes, art projects, and listening stations to pull out when they want (or NEED) a diversion in their day or when you need them to redirect their energy!

Converse...even if they don't understand.
Use big-for-them words. Show them calendars and clocks. Point out things as you drive. And even if they seem uninterested or unable to comprehend, keep doing it! They may not retain the information (but I think you will be surprised by how much they do learn), but they will retain the knowledge that mom likes them enough to talk to them...and that is an open door you want to keep open their entire lives!

CHAPTER 7

Meal Time

Meal Time

Having a table full of little ones can make meal time rather inter-esting – and messy - and difficult - and stressful. I remember hearing how other families had great dinner conversation, and how they all pitched in to clean up after the meal, and I won-dered if it was true because I felt like I was up to my armpits in chaos.

But now, as a mom who has made it further along in this jour-ney, I can honestly say meals do get easier, calmer, and even fun! But for those of you still in the trenches of only littles, let me give you some tips to make meal time the best it can be.

First of all, give yourself and your children some grace. They are little after all, and often they are simply behaving exactly the way little ones behave. Don't put expectations on them that are not attainable at their age. And don't beat yourself up because you are such a bad parent for not having your child trained to sit nicely at the table after a couple of tries. It takes time. It takes patience. And sometimes, it takes a few years.

Tip #1 – Set a Meal Reminder Timer
I wish I had learned this long ago! I now use my phone to tell me when to stop what I am doing and get going on dinner. When you have only little ones, you may need to do this for lunch and dinner (and perhaps even snack time!). The reason this is crucial is because hungry tummies become crazy kids in the blink of an eye. Moms are busy people, and need a reminder to stop what they are doing and attend to those hungry tum-mies before it gets out of hand.

CHAPTER 7

Tip #2 – Use Kid-Friendly Dinnerware
When you use kid-friendly dinnerware you not only save yourself the hassle of broken plates and cups, you also gain the opportunity to have your children start helping with table chores at a much younger age.

Tip #3 – Expect Spills
Seriously – why in the world do we get in such a huff when our kids spill something? They don't have the manual dexterity we adults have, and guess what, I still spill things! Don't fill the glasses too full. Keep an eye on how the kids are sitting and where their plates are, but the absolute best thing you can do is keep a dry rag handy right there at the table. In fact, if you use washcloth napkins like we do, your dry rag is already there!

Tip #4 – Keep Kids in High Chairs as Long as Possible
OK, so I don't mean until they fall asleep (although that does happen from time to time). What I mean is don't move kids to regular chairs until you absolutely have to.

Most of the dining rooms in the houses we've lived in only accommodated 1 high chair at a time, but if you can manage it, keep kids in high chairs as long as you can. It greatly minimizes the messes and the chaos. Children are contained and easier to control when they are confined to a high chair. You can also buy "high chairs" that hook to the table if you do not have room for extra high chairs in your dining room.

Meal Time

And I highly recommend you bring your littlest ones to the table in a high chair as soon as possible. We have a high chair that reclines so that even our smallest babies can join us at meal time.

Tip #5 – Create Meal Time Traditions that Make Sense
In our household, we typically serve from the table (unless it is a meal that has a lot of components – like tacos – that are better off served buffet style). The reason for this is that it keeps mom and dad from getting up multiple times throughout the meal, and it doesn't tempt the children to leave the table as well. (Helpful Hint: If you don't have a lot of room on your table, try using a rolling cart to keep the food nearby.)

We dish out the meal to the youngest ones to let it start cooling, and keep the plates near us as we pray so no one is eating while we pray.

Prayers are short because young children do not understand why they can't eat. If you want to do family devotions or a more in-depth Bible time, do it while they eat – they will be much more attentive.

Other meal time traditions that work well for little ones include singing a short song before or after the meal, having older ones help set the table, and making small talk that revolves around the food on their plate (remember, distracting a small child from their food usually means they quit paying attention to their food and subsequently, quit eating it). You can point out colors of food, ask them to find certain things on their plate, and ask them about the taste of the different foods.

Tip #6 – Discipline in Short, Sensible Segments
Unfortunately, you are going to have to discipline at the table from time to time (or maybe every time for a while). Here are a few of the behaviors we've had to discipline over the years and how we handled them:

- 1 year old willfully screaming in high chair – Turn high chair around, facing away from everyone. Tell the 1 year old you will turn it back around when they stop. The second they stop, turn them back around. If they persist, scoot them out of the room in the high chair, still facing away from table, and explain again that as soon as they stop, they will be promptly scooted back in. Rarely have we had a situation persist beyond this, but the couple of times we have, I took the baby out of the high chair and away from the dining room completely so that everyone else could eat in peace while I worked to calm the child. And yes, sometimes that child didn't get much of a dinner – and I had to eat mine later. But, like I said, this has been rare.

- 3 year old not sitting in seat – This is pretty simple. Keep reminding them to sit. Make sure their chair is straight with the table, so it is harder to get up, and consider keeping that child near an adult to nip the standing in the bud as quickly as possible. Our son who did this wasn't trying to be defiant, he just liked to keep moving and fidgeting, and that almost always resulted in him standing up at some point during the meal.

Meal Time

- Picky eater – I have to admit, we haven't had many picky eaters, but I think that is because I just don't allow it. I absolutely understand not liking certain foods, but in our house, you have to try a bite before you declare it unfit for human consumption. And you are never, ever allowed to be loud and obnoxious about the fact that you don't like something because that sort of nonsense influences other children and makes for a very rude houseguest when you eat at someone else's table. Choosing to fuss will only get you more bites of the food you don't like before you can be finished.

There was one time we had a child who would not eat his oatmeal, so he ended up sitting at the table, slowly spooning in bites until he finally finished it an hour later. However, looking back, I wouldn't do that again. I would let him try it and if he chose not to eat it, so be it. But, there wouldn't be anything else to eat until the next meal.

I will say that feeding your children a varied and unprocessed diet from the beginning will help tremendously with lessening the pickiness.

Tip #7 – Make Meal Time a Feast!
This may sound crazy, but I don't mean make elaborate meals and have a big ole celebration every time you eat. I mean make meal time a fun time! Do your very best to put on a happy face and take time to smile at your babies. Talk and joke and laugh! Make a special drink or dessert on occasion. Let the kids bring a stuffed animal to the table as a guest. Be a family and try

CHAPTER 7

very hard to enjoy this time.

Right now, this is the family you have. No, they aren't big. No, the conversation isn't riveting. Yes, you spend a lot of time managing the chaos, but some day you will look back on it all and smile as the rose-colored glasses of veteran motherhood make you believe "those were the good old days."

And frankly, they are. You are surrounded by chubby cherub faces who have no other place to be except sitting with you at the table. Cherish this moment – chaos and all.

CHAPTER 8

Snack Time

CHAPTER 8

Depending on your routine, snack time could happen anywhere from 1-3 times a day. In our home, it is usually 1 time a day with another snack in the evening on the weekends when we let the kids stay up a bit later.

Whatever your choice is on the number of snacks, having a set time for Snack Time is always a good idea. It gives stability to your day and your children's eating habits.

For us, Snack Time is 3:00 pm every day. I always try to keep fresh fruit on hand that can easily be eaten by little ones - apples that can be cut up, berries, bananas, clementines. I have an array of crackers and cheese, veggies like baby carrots, cucumbers, and radishes, as well as the occasional homemade treat. We mostly drink water and milk here, so Snack Time is usually water unless an older sister has made a pitcher of lemonade.

I like to keep plastic cups, plates, bowls, and kid-friendly flatware in a lower cabinet so they can help to get their own snacks. Most of these I have purchased from Ikea on Amazon.

This is a good time of day for a read-aloud! Sit at the table with them and read aloud from a favorite story book or themed book if you are working on a topic during learning time or it is near a holiday.

After they have eaten, have them help you clear the table and put away the snack things. After Snack Time, it's time to play!

CHAPTER 9

Play Time

CHAPTER 9

It may seem odd to have regular Play times, but I think it is important to have a good grasp of the activities you are doing with and for your children and the activities you are simply letting them do on their own. With that said, I find that Play Time falls into two categories:

1.) Free Time
and
2.) Organized Play

Free Time is when you allow your children to play with whatever they want however they want to play with it (within reason, of course). I like to have open-ended playthings for my children because I feel it fosters the most creativity and imagination. Examples would be dress-up clothes, LEGOs, blocks, kitchen toys, simple doll houses, little animals, baby dolls, and cars.

Free Time here occurs at natural intervals throughout the day - first thing when they wake up, after lunch, before supper, right before bedtime. It isn't scheduled or organized and the toys are readily accessible.

Organized Play, on the other hand, is just that...organized...by you or by another mom. It is often educational in nature, involves some prep work by whoever is leading the activity, and usually has intentions behind it like teaching a new skill, supplementing a learning lesson, or corresponding with a set of activities.

Play Time

Organized Play is MUCH more mommy-intensive, so I would caution you to only do as much as you can reasonably handle and allow the majority of your children's play time to be Free Time.

When your children are very young, a once-a-week time of Organized Play is all I would recommend. Start yourself a Pinterest board to gather ideas, choose one a week, and call it good.

As they get older, you may want to incorporate holiday activities or other themes while throwing in something resembling preschool (see the Learning Time section of this ebook!).

My littles ones are 9 months, 2, and 4. I do very little Organized Play with my 2 little girls, but while they nap, I do organized activities with my 4 year old which makes it much more manageable for me.

I usually keep a calendar or list of ideas to pull from, and I have a basket full of supplies for these activities. This makes it easier for me to gather the Organized Play Time things and get right into the activity. A small laundry basket or wooden basket is perfect for keeping your playthings organized.

Our Play Time occurs everywhere from the kitchen table to the living room to outdoors. It often rotates around a certain theme and usually there is a read-aloud book involved.

However you choose to organize this kind of play time, keep it

CHAPTER 9

simple and low-key. Let your children guide you on how long they can handle an activity, and stop before they are worn out. I would also suggest you do Organized Play Time on a schedule - every day at 2pm or Mondays at 10am for example. This gives you a guideline to offer your children when they incessantly ask you when it's time to do Play Time with you!

CHAPTER 10

Bible Time

CHAPTER 10

Take a moment to pause because I'm getting ready to tell you something important and I want you to be in the right mindset to hear it...

I'm going to challenge you to reconsider the typical handling of Bible Time with little ones.

So often, we stick to stories of Adam and Eve, Noah and the ark, Joseph and his coat, and never dig much deeper into the Word of God with our little ones because we don't believe they can handle much more than that. However, I have witnessed over the years very small children who are very capable of understanding much deeper truths and feasting on God's Word far beyond the typical preschool story books.

Don't underestimate your little ones!

Definitely give them the foundation of the well-known Bible stories, but honestly, if your child goes to Sunday School or watches anything Bible-related for kids on television, they already have a pretty solid foundation there. Don't waste your time rehashing the usual – get to the meat!

Let them know God had a plan from the beginning, and that plan was Jesus! Let them know that every story points to Jesus! Read deep Bible story books like Mighty Acts of God by Starr Meade, The Child's Story Bible by Catherine Vos, and The Jesus Storybook Bible by Sally Lloyd-Jones.

Bible Time

As you read to them, take note of how you can weave the truths of the Bible into your everyday life. When they disobey, let them know there are consequences and there is grace. When they don't want to share, remind them of how as Christ followers we are to share all that we have. When they are sad, help them to remember that the Lord bottles all their tears and is sad right along with them, but is always there to bring them back to rejoicing. Don't miss the opportunity to speak Christ into their everyday lives! They may be little, but they are the Kingdom of Heaven!

Because I have older children and we homeschool, our Bible Time fits neatly at the beginning of our school day. We also try to find the time to have Family Worship at night with singing and reading and praying.

You might want to put Bible Time first thing in the morning - Bible & Breakfast, anyone? Or you could read before naps or right after. Some parents like to linger at the dinner table longer and read then. Come up with a time and a place that works for your family and then put your Story Bible there. Set a reminder on your phone, and start discipling these little ones!

CHAPTER 11

Read Aloud Time

Bible Time

Read aloud time with little ones can be the most rewarding and most frustrating part of your day! Let me paint you a picture and give you some ideas for making Read Aloud Time something you look forward to...

We've all seen the peaceful paintings of a mother and a couple of children sitting down in a comfy chair to enjoy a special time of mother reading aloud. Yet, when we try to gather our brood for a beautiful moment of storybooks and snuggling, we end up breaking up kick fights and raising our voices to a painful screech in order to be heard over the chatter. We spend so much time fielding nonsensical questions and bouncing the baby so she will quiet down that we give up the whole fiasco only a few pages into the book. For days (and sometimes weeks), we avoid read aloud time altogether until we can no longer resist the siren song of those scrumptious pages and our unrealistic dreams of oil painting perfect afternoons. Once again, we seat the children around us and once again we are met with the same result.

It's time to change your motivation and your methods! It's time to make peace with Read Aloud Time!

When I only had two children, I could make Read Aloud Time look much like the painting I described above...for about 10 minutes. My curious son would soon begin asking questions, and my high needs daughter was soon overstimulated and needed a break. Fast forward a few years and a few kids, and I couldn't make Read Aloud Time look like anything picturesque. Thankfully, I quickly stopped beating myself up and began to mold Read Aloud Time into something that worked for our family.

So, let's get honest here...
Are you doing Read Alouds because someone said you "had to?" Do you feel guilty if you don't get them in? Are you longing for the ideal image you have in your head of what Read Aloud Time looks like?

STOP IT RIGHT NOW!
Your motivation for reading aloud to your children needs to change in order for you to find peace. Read to your children to introduce them to classics, help them calm down in the midst of a busy day, learn about a certain school subject, and enjoy a little bit of time together in fellowship.

Reading aloud doesn't require a certain amount of time in order for it to be legit. And it doesn't require a certain atmosphere in order for it to "count."

Something else I want to say here may differ from the opinions of others, but I do not believe Read Aloud Time should ever be a time of discipline. I know many people advocate for Read Aloud Time to be a time of teaching your children to sit still, but I don't want to bring that kind of strife into the equation. I would rather carve out another time to discipline my way through teaching a child to sit. If I have an antsy or disruptive little one, I either let them run off to play in another room or I wait to do read alouds until they are occupied elsewhere, sleeping, or in a better mood.

Bible Time

The surest way to make read alouds miserable is to spend the entire time disciplining.

So, let's get practical with the WHERE of reading aloud. Contrary to all those images of Read Aloud Time in your brain, you do not have to sit surrounded by your children in a floral chair near a window and a vase of flowers with soft music playing in the background. Read aloud time can have many homes and can change from day to day!

Here are a few ideas to get your started:
- at the dining room table after a meal
- at the table during the meal
- in the car on a trip
- in the car while waiting for Daddy to run an errand
- on the floor
- on the porch swing
- on the back porch
- on a blanket in the yard
- on the couch with the children on the floor
- *on the couch with some of the children on the back of the couch
- in your bed
- in the children's bedrooms with them in bed
- at the doctor's office
- in the bathtub (the kids, not you!)

One of the keys to WHERE is to have a book with you at all times and in all places where an impromptu Read Aloud Time might happen. I have books in every room of the house for this very reason!

So, what about the WHEN?

Frankly, the when can happen any time of day or night! Don't feel you have to be locked into a certain time. Life happens and feeling guilty because you didn't do your Read Aloud first thing in the morning makes for a rotten parenting day. And don't think you have to read aloud EVERY day in order to be a proper mom. Yes, it is good to shoot for a certain time each day (the children become accustomed to it and respond very well to that kind of rhythm), but your motivation for reading aloud is not to check off a box on your list. And remember, you don't have to read aloud for an hour or even half an hour. 10-15 minutes is well worth it and often has you stopping before any of the children begin to fall apart and lose interest.

Now, WHAT should you read aloud?

At the risk of sounding trite, my answer has to be ANYTHING! Read from the Bible itself, a book of Bible stories, a newspaper, the internet, Dr. Suess books, a book of poems, a Beatrix Potter anthology, a cookbook, the manual to your coffee pot.

Why?

Because reading aloud from a variety of sources gives your children exposure to many different words and styles of writing.

Read Aloud Time

Take them to museums and read the plaques. Read billboards as you are driving. Read mail, magazine articles, and backs of cereal boxes!

Yes, I know that isn't quite the answer you were looking for, but the more you can expose your children to the written word, the more they will acquire a taste for it and an understanding of sentence structure and vocabulary.

But, if you are looking for a list of books, I do have a few suggestions...

- *Honey for a Child's Heart* by Gladys Hunt
- Homeschool curriculum book lists (try lists from Sonlight, Tapestry of Grace, Heart of Dakota, or Ambleside Online)
- Do a search on Pinterest for books lists by age and stage or theme

Trust me when I say that someday you will look back on your little family's Read Aloud Time and smile because you will no longer remember all the craziness and chaos or the times you didn't fit it into your day, or the child who never sat still. You will only remember with a sigh and a smile and those lovely rose-colored glasses history hands you how Read Aloud Time felt like your own little slice of Heaven.

CHAPTER 12

Outside Time

Outside Time

When you only have 1 or 2 little ones, Outside Time doesn't seem that difficult to manage, but add in 1 or 2 more, and it suddenly becomes exponentially harder to keep everyone safe and in sight! But, we all know our kiddos should get outside and breathe in fresh air and sunshine while learning to revel in God's creation. Here are a few tips to manage Outside Time when you have more kids than hands...

- **Fence in your yard or an area of your yard.** - You will feel a lot more in control if you have a safety net - namely a fence - in place. Some houses we've lived in had fenced backyards and some did not. While we could not afford to fence in the entire yard or were not allowed to because it was a rental, we were able to afford and put up a small amount of fencing with a gate that served as a safe area to play. If you have wanderers, this will make for much less stressful outside play!

- **Set up a Central Command**. - In my backyard, this is the table on the patio, but in a park setting, this could be a blanket, a cooler, or anything that signifies your domain and contains all the extras you might need. If you are on a walk with the children, this would be a backpack or the basket of the stroller. Not only is it where you keep diapers, wipes, extra clothes, water bottles, sunscreen, etc, it is an easily identifiable landmark for your children to come to when called, to go to when they need something, or to stay near if Mommy needs to tend to another sibling. It provides you with a place to put everything and an area to gather the children.

- **Teach your children to "hang on."** - Whether it is a stroller or a grocery cart or your hand, small children need to learn the importance of hanging on. This is especially important on walks or in large crowds. You might even want to tie short ropes to your stroller for this purpose. Teach them that the words "hang on" or simply "cart" or "stroller" mean they need to immediately grab on and stay there. This is something I implemented when I used to take my little ones shopping with me. I would say, "Cart," and they knew it meant grab on to the cart and stay there as we walk so that I didn't lose them and they didn't get in the way of other people.

- **Balance organized outside play and free play.** - Just as we talked about in the Play Time chapter, Outside Time should have the same balance. It is not your job to entertain your children outside. Certainly, play ball with them or push them on the swings, but there is no need for you to initiate every single outdoor activity. When you have a lot of littles, it is quite likely you are either pregnant or have a baby in a stroller or wrap (or both!) making it nearly impossible for you to manage every aspect of the other children's Outside Time. Children are highly creative if you simply let them be!

- **Facilitate outdoor play with open-ended toys**. - In the name of creativity, consider what items you can have on hand specifically for Outside Time. We keep a nature bag by our backdoor. It has binoculars, magnifying glasses, nature books, and bug dens. We have a waterproof blanket that sits near the backdoor as well, ready to be spread out on the lawn for

Waterproof blanket!

an impromptu look at clouds or stars or autumn leaves. We have an old plastic kitchen set for pretending to cook with leaves and grass, and plenty of trowels and buckets for digging (yes, I let my kids dig in certain designated areas of the yard). On various occasions, we use sidewalk chalk, balls, frisbees, bubbles, and water balloons. Keep these items in a special place just for outdoor toys, and you'll be ready for Outside Time in a jiffy!

- **Get a whistle or bell.** - Years ago, I purchased an old school bell from an antique shop to use for calling the children in from outside or even from their various locations within the house. I have a friend who keeps a whistle around her neck like Captain von Trapp for calling her children to her in crowds. Even very small children can become accustomed to coming when "called" by a bell or whistle and it saves your voice!

- **Dress them alike when you are away from home for Outside Time**. - If your Outside Time is going to be spent on a Nature Walk or at a park, consider dressing all of the children in a bright color so they can easily be spotted. Orange was often our color of choice when my children were little. It didn't blend in with surroundings, and I knew exactly what my children were dressed in should the awful need to give a description of them ever arise.

CHAPTER 13

Rainy Days

Rainy Days

When the weather outside is frightful, many a mom of littles
finds the indoors to be just as frightful! Little ones who feel
cooped up can quickly become unruly, and mama can quickly
come undone. But with a little imagination, bad weather can
become your best friend!

The trick to handling little ones who are forced to stay inside all
day is to consider inclement weather to be an invitation to adventure! These are the days when the schedule loosens and the
fun begins. Here are a few ideas to help you see how wonderful
rainy days (and snowy days and everything in between) can be!

- **Build a Fort** - a small table, a couple of chairs, a pile of blankets, and you have endless hours of fun! Gather stuffed
  animals and books for a special reading cave. Eat snacks
  and watch a favorite movie for an afternoon treat. Pile pillows and blankets inside and let them sleep there for naps
  or even overnight! You might even want to spring for some
  battery-operated fairy lights to make their space even more
  magical!

- **Garage Sale Game** - When I was kid, rainy days were garage
  sale days! No, my mom and I weren't out galavanting across
  the city finding deals. Rather, I was dragging out my toys
  and "selling" them to her! Cut up some slips of paper for
  price tags, grab some monopoly money (or the real stuff!),
  and get to shopping, mama!

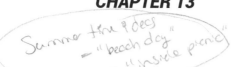

Summer time & decs
- "beach day"
- "inside picnic"

Fall/Winter
- obstacle course
- gymnastics
- forts/top

- **Have a Feast** - Perhaps it is because I actually love rain and snow that I find myself wanting to throw a feast when those days come. No matter how you feel about the weather, when it keeps your kids indoors, have a feast! Little people are easily impressed, so your feast can be a bag of frozen meatballs cooked up and a block of cheese cut into squares and toothpicks as utensils. You can eat on pillows on the floor or use tray tables on the couch. On snowy days, make snowball cookies and drink hot cocoa. Make breakfast for supper, have an ice cream sundae bar, a baked potato bar, a taco bar! Have a progressive supper where food is placed in different rooms and you go from room to room taste testing. The possibilities are endless!

- **Have a Movie-Themed Day** - Watch Cloudy with a Chance of Meatballs and eat spaghetti. Have a Grinch Party where you watch the How the Grinch Stole Christmas! and eat Who Hash and Roast Beast. Watch Up while sitting in a laundry basket with helium balloons tied to it (you can get helium balloons at many dollar stores for $1 a piece!). Google "Movie Themed Party for Kids" and see just how many great ideas are floating around out there!

- **Rainy Day Box** - Have a special box that is only brought out on bad weather days. It can be a big box of blocks or other long-lasting toy, or it can be a few small toys that are special because they aren't overplayed with. For instance, something like play dough or floam, a box of wooden train tracks or a dollhouse. Anything that doesn't get played with often!

Puddle Jumping - When you can, let your children go out and enjoy the rain (or at the very least, the aftermath of the rain). Yes, it's a muddy mess, but mud is the stuff of memories! Keep mud boots in the garage and junk towels in the closet for this very occasion. It doesn't have to be every time it rains, but don't be afraid to let your kids be kids! For snow days, keep a tub of snow clothes on hand that makes it easy for you to line them up, dress them, and send them out to play. Keep those same junk towels on hand for them to step on when they come into the house and derobe.

Live the Adventure!

Daily outside

- Summer 20 min each time in heat or sun
- early morning play, evening "stroll"? or outside
  + park?

CHAPTER 14

Birthdays & Holidays

Birthdays & Holidays

When you have a lot of little ones birthdays and holidays can feel super special and also super stressful. This chapter will give you ideas for taking the stress out of birthdays and holidays for good!

First of all, if you are putting together mega birthday parties that cater to the people attending rather than to your child, STOP IT RIGHT NOW! Birthday parties are NOT for the attendees. They are to celebrate the anniversary of YOUR CHILD'S birth! Whoever started the insane tradition of giving the attendees all sorts of gifts and feeding them gourmet meals and incredibly elaborate cake probably only had one child.

In our family, we stopped celebrating birthdays with lots of friends and family when our second child was little. She hated having lots of people around making a fuss, and so we stopped out of necessity. However, I'm not the least bit sorry to no longer have to plan formal birthday parties. Only our older children celebrate with friends, and usually only one friend at that.

Our favorite way to celebrate birthdays now is to have a big to-do with just our family and sometimes a grandparent or two. The birthday child gets to choose the food for the day and the kind of cake (or birthday dessert for those who aren't fond of cake). They also get off from chores the week of their birthday. We fuss over them and serve them all day long. It's the best day of the year for the birthday kid!

CHAPTER 14

If you actually enjoy planning friend birthday parties, remember that low-key is always more fun because mom isn't stressed! Don't over-schedule games, food, and present time. No one cares about elaborate decorations, so spend your money else-where. Consider going with a theme that is unique and simple. For instance, a hot chocolate bar, a tea party, or a teddy bear picnic are all ideas that can easily be implemented and are fun because they aren't done all the time.

And remember to consider YOUR child above all else. What do they like? What are their interests? How can you honor THEM in the celebrations?

This is also a great time to teach your other children servant-hood and hospitality. The birthday child is the center of atten-tion and that's the way it should be. We don't coddle a child who feels "left out." Rather, we gently remind them that their turn is coming up, and they will be treated like a king or queen on their day. Encourage them to treat their sibling exactly the way they would like to be treated. You don't have to overdo it, and you shouldn't spend a lot of time talking about it because that detracts from the celebrations, but do address it swiftly and then get back to the party.

As for presents, keep them thoughtful. No one needs a lot of stuff. Focus on experiences and open-ended play. Take your child to the zoo or discovery center for their birthday in lieu of a gift. Give them lessons or day trips as a way to create lasting experiences. If you decide to give gifts, make sure they are things your child will really play with and something you are willing to have in your house for years to come. Also, make sure they allow for imagination and lots of variety of play.

For holidays, my advice would be very similar. Make memories with food, movies, activities, and outings that don't cause stress. Celebrate the real reason behind each holiday, and keep things low-key and meaningful.

CHAPTER 15

Quality Time

Quality Time

The one question I hear most from moms of many littles is how to find the hours in the day to spend quality time with each of their children. Life can feel like a perpetual putting out of fires when you have a lot of littles, and putting out fires is very time consuming.

Hopefully, prior to this chapter, you have found some ways to lessen the amount of fires in your day, so that you can redeem some time to spend just being with your kiddos. But, even if you skipped right to this chapter, I want to offer you some super practical ideas for having enough of you to go around that will at least get you headed in the right direction.

Tip #1 - Delegate

I am the manager of my home and good managers ALWAYS delegate responsibilities.

Moms have this notion they should be able to do everything and be everything to everybody. If I try that approach my children will one day remember me as the mom who was always too busy. Not an epitaph to be particularly proud of.

But, who do I delegate to?

If grandparents are nearby, they are great for those little extras that are hard to fit into a day. They can read to the children, host tea parties, take them on field trips, even just take one or two for the day to give you time and space to do something you've been needing to do with the others. If you have other relatives nearby, you could easily delegate to them as well. The biggest thing to keep in mind when handing off some of your responsibilities to relatives is to delegate things they find enjoyable or have an aptitude for. In other words, don't ask Grandpa to wash the 2 year old's hair (unless he's actually good at it!).

Then there are the children themselves. It is important to <u>give the children responsibilities</u> as they age. I have a couple of budding cooks who have a couple of meals a week that are theirs to prepare. It's nothing fancy, but it's a start. They get the opportunity to learn and mature and I get a couple of hours I can redeem and redistribute elsewhere.

How about Dad? There are many women who complain about Dad not pitching in with things, but men aren't always in tune with the family's day-to-day life and need a little briefing on where they can pitch in at. Perhaps Dad can help out with special projects, giving the toddler a bath, or cooking a meal once a week. Don't be pushy, but do ask. And don't forget to bounce ideas off of him when you are feeling overwhelmed. Brainstorm with him ways you can hand off some of the load you carry.

Tip #2 - Eliminate your time wasters

Quality Time

Consider what unnecessary things are eating your time. My time wasters have changed over the years. Once upon a time, it was sewing. Another season in life it was reading. And of course, there is always the big, bad internet! All of these (and more) have at some point in my life taken time away from my family. So, if you feel crunched for time, then there's a good chance there is something in your life that needs to go.

Time wasters aren't always bad things, but they aren't always the best things. We have to practice a little self-denial and walk away from those things for a season. Prioritize what is import-ant and avoid the rest.

Tip #3 - Don't let the schedule rule you

Not that schedules are bad, but sometimes they tie your hands. If your husband needs you to take care of something on Tues-day that you would normally take care of on Thursday and you feel you cannot deviate from your schedule, you will only end up feeling out of sorts, anxious, and grumpy.

Everyone knows a good schedule can actually add time to your day; however, you have to be flexible in order to take care of off-schedule items.
When you have off-schedule items, make a list of those things and work through the list in an orderly fashion, making the rest

of your schedule fit around the list.

Avoid throwing the schedule out completely because I have found every single day has its share of off-schedule items. If you start throwing out your schedule every time you have something extra to fit in, you'll never work your schedule and you'll always feel off track. So, give yourself a little margin in your day to allow for off-schedule items to be fit in as needed.

Tip #4 - Institute a Special Night for each child

As our family grew, I realized Daddy and I weren't always connecting on a deeper level with each of the kids. To remedy this, we instituted what we call Special Night. Every week on Tuesday, one of our children is the "Special Child" who gets to stay up later, pick a snack and drink for the evening, and choose special activities to do with mom and dad. It gives us a chance to get to know our children individually, learn their interests, and make them feel super special!

Tip #5 - Family first

We have a rule of thumb in this house. If it doesn't benefit the family, it's not worth doing. That means if one or more of us participates in an activity that begins to show signs of tearing away at the family's infrastructure, it needs to go...sooner, rather than later. In fact, it is best to assess an activity prior to participation because it is much harder to walk away from something once you've been involved in it for a while. Always remember, there will never be enough of you to go around if all you do is run around.

We also try to make the majority of our activities things the entire family can enjoy. This isn't possible in everything, but the more things you do as a family unit, the easier it is to meet everyone's needs as a mama.

Tip #6 - Character doesn't come from the easy life

Perhaps you think there isn't enough of you to go around because your children don't have the best of everything, the perfect day, their heart's desire every single moment of their little lives. Giving your children everything they want all the time will not build the strength of character they will need to be leaders in this world. They must understand through experience that the world does not revolve around them.

I am one person, and there are moments during the day when I have to choose one child over another. Not out of favoritism, but because wiping a little one's bum is more necessary than sharpening another one's pencil. I do my children a disservice if I try to pretend I'm some superwoman, there to do their bidding all day long. Patience, deference, humility and the likes are born out of hardship. Not that I want my children to have a hard life, but I shouldn't want them to have an easy life either.

Tip #7 - Slow down and relax

Savor that cup of tea, breathe that fresh air, smile more. Take naps with the kids, build forts out of blankets, have a conversation with a 5 year old. So often, you will feel the most stressed when you are trying to move too fast. It's time to slow down. If you are feeling worn thin then you probably are.

God wants you to rest. He expects you to be still. He created you. He knows your circumstances. Let Him order your day. He called you to this.
He will equip you for this. God's ways aren't always my ways, but God is always right.

In order to have enough of me to go around, I have to let go of some of my expectations. I have to let God lead. I have to be content with his Light only shining on my very next step, rather than the entire path. Only then will I be the mom I need to be.

If I'm caught up in what I think or what the world thinks or what my next-door neighbor thinks, I'll never find the freedom to live my life based on what God thinks. I'll never take the time just to walk in the park and sing silly songs with my kids. I'll never ask all of my littles to join me in the kitchen to make cookies. I'll never watch my nursling sleep in my arms.

Quality Time

There really isn't enough of me to go around. I am one person and I cannot possibly do it all. But God hasn't asked me to do it all. He's asked me to give my all...to Him. He'll order my life from there. All I have to do is live it. Yes, it is hard, but when you look around at these little faces looking up at you, you cannot help but see how beautiful all of this is.

That is the essence of this life with littles. They are only little once. Even when you have a house full of little ones, they don't stay that way.

It is true...
So many littles, yet so little time.

BONUS CONTENT

There's a New Baby!

There's a New Baby!
a toddler's guide to managing the transition

One thing a mom of many little ones knows is that babies don't stay babies long, and toddlers who were once the baby don't get to be the baby forever. I am often asked how I handle sibling rivalry, and my short answer is that it doesn't happen here. But, I know that's not really a good enough answer for moms who are either afraid they will have to deal with it or who are actually dealing with it and can't figure out how to get the situation resolved without damaging little psyches.

This is my honest assessment of sibling jealousy, and how it should be handled. You may not agree with me, but at least hear me out.

Sibling jealousy is often nurtured

Sometimes it comes from mom and dad, sometimes a well-meaning grandparent, sometimes from Joe Schmoe down the street. Someone says something that seems harmless and the little kid wheels start turning.

For instance, Grandma tells little Timmy that when his new baby sister is born he might feel like he's not getting any attention, but his parents really do love him.

Hello?! Let's just set the little guy up for failure, shall we?

Or what about mom and dad who bend over backward to try to

keep little Timmy from feeling jealous with presents and coddling. Or maybe the opposite happens, and mom and dad suddenly focus all their attention on this tiny creature, all the while making it very clear that Timmy is "in the way".

Don't encourage jealousy with your words and actions. As adults, we are the ones these little people take their cues from. If your cues are suggesting they *should* be jealous of a new baby, then they *will* be jealous.

Jealousy stems from confusion

We have always made the new baby a part of the family from the time he or she is a tiny little bump in mama's belly. The baby is an addition, not a replacement, and our children are encouraged to dream about baby, shop for baby, talk about baby, and ask questions about baby long before the baby joins the family on the outside.

If you avoid talking about baby and letting your little ones interact with the baby before he or she is born, you end up surprising your child with a kicking, screaming doll that is terrifying. Mom and Dad spend a lot of time dealing with this tiny human, and little Timmy is totally confused about who this person is and how he is supposed to interact if he's never been told this baby is "his" too.

There's a New Baby!
a toddler's guide to managing the transition

Yes, your child may be too young to understand, but don't let that stop you from talking about baby and including your child in baby related activities like shopping for baby and baby showers.

Jealous siblings see the new baby as YOURS, not OURS

We talk about OUR baby. We tell our toddlers the new baby is THEIR baby. We make sure they know this new little one is a part of OUR family, and we talk about what it means to be a part of OUR family.

They come to the hospital. We encourage them to hold baby. We let them join in diaper changes, baths, and feeding. We are in this together, and baby is an addition to our family dynamic that we all get to enjoy.

But, if a parent excludes their other children from the day to day routine of having a new baby, or they never talk about baby being OUR baby, a toddler or older sibling may get the impression the baby isn't someone they should pay attention to or bond with.

All this said, my biggest gripe with this whole sibling jealousy thing is...

Sibling jealousy is talked about way too much

Any little sign of a child feeling jealous and we jump on the "we might warp them if we don't do something quick" bandwagon. We are so busy trying to nurture our poor jealous child's psyche, we end up making things worse! We run to grandparents, friends on Facebook, and even strangers in the supermarket to get their opinion on jealous siblings. All the while, our little children are wondering what you are so in a tizzy over, but the attention they are getting sure is fun! It doesn't matter if the perceived jealousy is real or not, if little Timmy can milk it, he will.

He may actually be feeling a little left out and confused by this new person in his home, but if you run around like a crazy person, stressing over everything he says and feels, he's not going to feel MORE secure, he's going to wonder what is going on and act out even more!

Stop talking about it so much!

Stop stressing over it!

Bring little Timmy alongside you and baby and show him that having a new baby in the house is just the way things are and everyone is better for it.

I truly believe many "modern" sibling issues are a lot of hype. We parents stress over everything it seems. Somehow we've got to get a grip and just be parents...be a family...have a life! No more majoring in the minors. Let's enjoy our families! **<u>Let's show them just how wonderful and special new babies are</u>.** Let's try to keep things low-key and normal. No more jealous sibling nonsense!

And now, I will step off my soapbox...

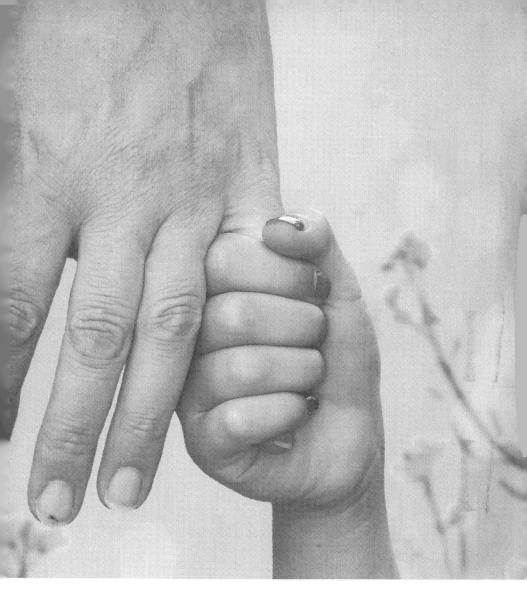

BONUS CONTENT

Cherish Your Children Checklist

Cherish Your Children Checklist

Click **here** to download!
or go to:
http://www.subscribepage.com/cherishchildren

Enjoy!

Please visit RaisingArrows.net for more great content and resources for moms of many littles. You can also send an email to me - amy@raisingarrows.net - if you have more questions!